PEN TO PAPER~
THOUGHTS UNEDITED

KAI MANN

Also By Kai Mann

30 Day Notice~ "The Eviction Chronicles part I"

Abandoned Property~ "The Eviction Chronicles part II"

PEN TO PAPER~
THOUGHTS UNEDITED

POETICALLY THINKING

KAI MANN

Scriblical Vibez Publishing

For information address
Scriblical Vibez Publishing
P O Box 06215
Plymouth, MI 48170-6215

Scriblical Vibez Publishing books may be purchased for educational,
business, or sales promotional use. For information please write: Sales
Department, Scriblical Vibez Publishing, P O Box 06215, Plymouth, MI
48170-6215.

First Edition

Designed by Pat Rasch

ISBN: 978-0-9848281-6-6

Thoughts Unedited: because words are paintings on pages
strategically placed even when out of place

CONTENTS

ACKNOWLEDGMENTS

I'd like to thank the Creator for the breath of life, of creativity, and of courage.

Stop telling people who you are
Show them

I'm good enough for me.

IT AIN'T ALL ME

When you're in tune with your destiny
All the things
You thought as coincidences
You know that it happened now
Like it was supposed to
You'll no longer be afraid
When you see signs thinking
"That's weird"
because you
Forgot that you placed
A question to the Universe
Because you weren't really expecting an answer
But now you do
And you get help
Everytime you ask
Sometimes I want to imagine
How that help looks
Then I realize that
Although I'm here
It ain't all me

RESPONSIBLE

Even though I wasn't there
I was still there.
I chose him for this reason
He was responsible

HE WATCHES WITH PRIDE

Slowly introduce yourself to the world
You don't have to do it
All at once
It's better this way
Give yourself the chance to see you
While others watch
"All things work together for them that love him"

I think seeking him
You find yourself
Not in a disrespectful way
But in a way that's
So open
A way that he watches
With pride

NEGATIVITY

I know how you don't want to
Hear nothing negative
About what you're doing
But
I don't know how long
That could last
Not because you
Want to
But
You know it's
Unavoidable
You'll have to hear it
One way
Or
another

LOVE

Love had me caught
It learned me some things
That I had never thought
Love had broken me down to the lowest denominator
Love had attacked me like the hardest perpetrator
Love had...
Love had me so gone that I didn't know which way was up
Once I thought that I had lost my peripheral vision
Love hit me like a head on collision
Love taught me a lesson
Love loved me so much that it was a blessing
Love can be tough
She can make it real easy
Or she could make it rough

BECAUSE I CAN

I'm going to write through it all
I'm going to write through the pain
Through the happiness
And through the rain

I'm going to write just because I can

SOMEONE ELSE

Life doesn't have to be so hard
You don't have to make it harder on yourself
But I don't know if you learned more from that
Or less
And if it had to take the length of time that it did
But it did
So it must
Right?
You're everything
Made up of a lot of good
And a lot of sad
Not wrong, or even bad
You're made up of everything
You would be someone different
If you made a different decision
In at any time
You could've been
A couple of different people
But I think
That isn't who you weren't meant to be
Because if not
You would've been someone else

THAT'S ALL YOU NEED

These are just my thoughts
It's not like I don't have anyone to share them with
I just am choosy about who
I do
Everything isn't for everybody
Only some people
Will get you
Just a few
But you're going to be alright
Because that's
All you'll need

PAY ATTENTION

Pay attention to things people say to you
Hear their words
I'm learning to hear them
From the inside out
I don't care about
What's going on the outside
Only what's going on in the inside
Sometimes spirits come in place of chatter
They make noise
And you have to learn
How to not listen
If you listen you get distracted
And thrown off of the path
So pay attention

PARABLES

I know why he did it
He spoke in parables
Because it's a mystery
And you have to be willing
to go after *it*
to solve *it*

WILLING

It can be done
You just have to be willing
To do it
Whatever "it" is
You fill in the blank

HUMBLE

I see how it keeps you humble
You have different people
Telling you
Different things
And you need a balance of both
To keep you
Somewhere in the middle
Not someone to totally
Emasculate you
But not someone who just tells you anything
Either

FLOPS

If it flops
It just flops
At least you did something

IT'S TIME

Instead of saying
Who you don't want to be
Say who
You want to be
Challenge yourself
To find out
What that means to you
Being the best representation
Of who you are

It's time.....

PURPOSE

In six months I don't want to work for someone else
I want to work for you
And not have to worry
About anything
You've put my purpose
Inside me
And
I've found it

PAIN

Sometimes pain can be so definite
     And sometimes you don't know
Why it hurts
     Or even where
But the one thing that's for a fact
...You want it to stop

UNTIL IT HAPPENS

I think I've found what I'm supposed to do
Not in its entirety
But the surface of it
I don't know the magnitude of it
And I won't know for sure
Until it happens

CLOSER

If I can get close to God
I think I get
Closer to myself
I think I'll be my *best* self
I'm not sure how much
Some things matter
Or if anything does
But I think we let a lot
Get in the way
Stuff that doesn't matter
And even the stuff that does
If we only knew the meaning
Of the two

TRY

We are more powerful than we could have ever imagined
Our actions are weak
Because they don't know it
If you want to
You'll try

COMPARING

When you quit comparing
Who someone else is
To who you think
That's who you're supposed to be
You'll move forward
I don't know how far
But steps ahead
are good

EGO

Sometimes you can feel ego try to
Step in
It'll try to rear its little head
But you have to put it
In its place
That's not where
You're trying to go
You want the best
Possible outcome
And that's not it

Sometimes it gets harder
Because it'll try to find out
your weak spots
So it's important
That you always
Tell it the same thing
"No!"

IS IT WRONG

Does it make me wrong
Because I want to see
Something soft in front of me
Is it wrong for me
To want something sensual
Something I can love like I do
Is there something wrong
With that?

HOLD ON

I'm sorry we haven't laid together in awhile
I'm sorry I haven't caressed you in some time
I'm sorry baby

But...when I do
I want to hold on
And not have to let go

REFLECTIONS

I strategically placed mirrors
In the eyes
Of those souls
To reflect inspirations of hope
We feed from the same pond
To drink from
Each other's spirits
In remembrance of
Our existence
And purpose

MEAT

There are those who I look for
Not of wanting
But of knowing
Their souls connect with me
On a level just passed
Superficiality
To something more
I can count them on both hands
Their words feed my spirit
Leaving me not empty
But not quite full
Until next time
When I need to be fed thought
Or revelation
They come right on time
As if they can feel
The hunger
Or need for food
The hunter seeking
Meat

PAST THE SHALLOW END

It's really not that deep
It just seems that way
Rarely do we let our minds
Roam past the shallow end.

LIKE IT

If you don't like it
It's not for you

BETTER

It feels better
It feels better doing what you're comfortable doing
Not what you think you have to do
Trust me

AROUND YOU

Try doing what you feel
And see who says what
Anybody that says anything negative
Get them from around you
That's how you know who
Should be around you

STEPS BACKWARD

I messed up right there
I see it plain as day
When I did something
She wanted
that she said was me
And I hadn't done it before
But I knew it wasn't me
That's where I messed up
Because no matter what happened after that
I could've done whatever I wanted
And not felt forced to
There was no reason why you couldn't
Have stayed and fought
I wonder if I went a bunch of steps backwards
Before I went forward

TRUST YOURSELF

The Spirit knows which one is which
trust that

PURPOSELY

You ever hear a song
And you instantly
Go back to the place you were
When you were listening to that song
Not heard that song
But listened
heard suggests that it could've been
A few times
But listening implies
That you were doing so
Purposely

PROUD OF YOU

I'm proud of you
I think we all have a purpose
And I believe
You have found yours
Don't let anyone tell you
Anything different

GOD

God, you're too much sometimes...
For real

OLDER

It's hard doing something
You've never done before
The older you get

INTENT

To know the intent of the words
Are first to be known
If they shall be repeated, shared,
Or retweeted
Truth comes in many forms
And have many meanings
Depending upon
Receivership

TRUE

I write what I feel down to see if it is true
I dissect the words to make sure they are
In the write place
Until they are
True

EMOTION

For I know of sadness
And this is not that
I do have sorrow
I am full with emotion
Some known
And some
Unknown

SETBACK

The trouble is finding like minds
Everyone is not on the same page as you
And it's not always easy to tell
It's not wasted time
But it does set you back
A little

BEHIND

I know we say that everything happens as it should
But sometimes
I want it to happen better
Faster
Sometimes I think
I'm behind

DO BETTER

That statement is only half true
People who do better do
Because they know better
Not everyone who knows better
Does better

IT'S SHOWING

The effects are starting to show...

INSTINCTS

My instincts
Doesn't work like yours
You have to pay attention
So you can tell
What your spirit
Is telling you to do
When to do
And
How to do it

MAKE UP TIME

I think they'll get it in their time
I see it though
Its coming
There's a little light starting to show
Through the tunnel
They are so good though
Their hearts are all so pure
I feel it
When mine beats
Not together
But still one
Still four
Still us
Still love
Still two
We are the same
I see it at times
But just as I did
Got lost at some points
And came back
Had to do double time
Just to pick up time
So I could make up time

COULD YOU IMAGINE IT

You need someone to introduce you
Someone who believes so deeply in who you are
That when you speak
Their heart beats
When God shows me things
My heart beats
All the valves open up
And blood rushes through
So far that I loose
My breath
I have to hold my chest
It's so amazing to feel
I know that I've never
Felt that before
I was told that
It only gets better
I wonder if my head
Is going to pop off
Or what
Could you imagine it

I HOPE YOU DO

They won't understand
Few will
But
I'm gonna share it anyway
Hoping you do

THIS TIME

It's not a bit of arrogance
But those who don't get it
Or want to pick you apart
Don't sweat it because it's
Only the negative energy
Trying to get you
To go some place
Else
You don't have to go
You can do something different
This time...

MY GIRL DESERVES IT

She is everything that I didn't know that I wanted
She gives me hell
But she deserves it
So I can't say nothing
Have you ever had someone give you all of them
From the beginning
I've never had anyone just give it all to me
When she was there
She was in
And I believe she deserves it
It's been a little while
And she's gone through my not's
And my knots
That's why
When she comes home
And I'm downstairs
I meet her at the door
And I take her shoes off
Then her jacket
And later her scarf

She works hard
She's a good mother
And wife
I'm trying to enjoy it

And not worry about
What's going to happen
I just want to make sure
That I make it better
I have the option of doing that
And so do you

DO YOU

It is time
That you control your climate
You let some turn the knob up
And you get hot
You can go some place
You didn't want to go
But if you control the heat
Rather than letting them
You can enjoy
A lot longer
Don't worry
About them
Do you

I NEED HELP

You're not going to have to do something magical
I know that I'm going to have to do some stuff
So
I need some help

MY WORLD

Sometimes the world just opens up for me

And my chest

Expands

As air

Flows

Hastily

To the bottom

Of my lungs

It's so deep

That I breathe

Slow

As I write

I've had a long affair

With writing

My senses heighten

My nerves all

Are on edge

I feel them

When I move

JUMP

I'm going to do it
What's going to happen
If I don't
Why step to the edge
Peering over
Why not
Jump

AIR

Search for the air
When the climb gets higher
   realize that
when you step up
   to draw in air
As deep as you can
Just so you'll have enough
   to last you
you don't want to
Run out of air

WONDERMENT

There's a lot to this
      Don't be fooled
You have to stay
         You have to
Put enough
      Weight
In the ground
        To keep you
      Steady
So you won't just
        Lift off of
The ground
      But it's
Not
      Easy
I don't want you
        To think that
But that's why
      only
        Few make it

The air gets thinner
    And you've gotta
Be able
To breathe
        But once you do
Its pure wonderment
        Something you have never experienced
        Ever
And it'll fill your
        Lungs
With plenty
    Of air

EVERYTHING INTO YOU

The opportunity to have
Someone enjoy
and love you so much
that
They invest their
Everything
into
You

DREAMS

I just want to do some stuff
Don't you
What's the point of dreams
If they can't come
True...

WHAT SHE WANTS

I want her to have what
She wants
She deserves it
Her needs
Are already met

WHEN'S THE GOOD PART

I just want to get to the good part
Am I wrong?
I know it sounds like I'm rushing it
But man! Some of these issues are mind boggling
I just would've thought differently
I try to allow room for growth
But it's hard
Because this is simple...basic things
Nothing major
And it is wearing me out.
I am not lying
I know
For real though,
I gotta figure it out
Quick
Because I don't know
How much more I can take.
Lord Jesus,
What I gotta do?
I'd rather have more
Breathless days because of
Beauty

Tranquility...laughter....peace
And joy
I want all of that but
I'm a little afraid that as soon as I
Find it
It'll be gone
Including me
How nice it would be to just be happy
More than
Shocked...angered....
And just plain ole' frustrated
I've never been frustrated before
I thought I had felt
Every emotion there was
But I'm finding,
I'm not
I'm trying to work it out
So I can get to the next level
And learn
What I gotta learn
Because I want more
Maybe they're like I used to be
Didn't know there was more
Didn't even think about it
I was thinking for the moment
I don't want to do that no more

www.ingramcontent.com/pod-product-compliance
Lightning Source LLC
Chambersburg PA
CBHW071424040426
42445CB00012BA/1287